Safe
Connections

A Parent's Guide to Protecting Young Teens from Sexual Exploitation

by Sandy K. Wurtele, Ph.D.

PARENTING PRESS

Seattle | Washington

Printed in the United States of America
Designed by Magrit Baurecht (Core Creative Team)

ISBN 978-1-936903-00-9 paperback book
ISBN 978-1-936903-02-3 downloadable book at
www.ParentingPress.com

Library of Congress Cataloging-in-Publication Data
Wurtele, Sandy K. (Sandy Kay), 1955-
 Safe Connections : a parent's guide to protecting young teens
from sexual exploitation / by Sandy K. Wurtele.
  p. cm.
 Includes index.
 ISBN 978-1-936903-00-9 (pbk.) – ISBN 978-1-936903-02-3
(donwnloadable from publisher)
  1. Child sexual abuse–Prevention. 2. Sexually abused teenagers.
3. Sex crimes–Prevention. 4. Teenagers–Sexual behavior. 5.
Internet and teenagers. I. Title.
 HV6570.W873 2011
 649'.65–dc23

                                                 2011027192

Parenting Press
P.O. Box 75267
Seattle, Washington 98175

For more helpful publications and services for parents, caregivers,
and children, go to *www.ParentingPress.com*.

e

Contents

Introduction

Keeping children safe is priority number one for virtually all parents. Many parents, especially those raising "tweens" (pre-teenagers between 10 and 12) and young teens (13 to 15), also worry about their children's sexual safety as they start connecting romantically with others.

Today's tweens and teens face many risks as they seek out romantic connections both online and offline. What are some of these dangers?

- **Sexual abuse by adults.** According to the most reliable studies, as many as one out of eight boys and girls are sexually exploited by adults at some point during their childhood, with the highest rate among 12- to 15-year-olds.

- **Dating violence victim or offender.** While dating can be one of the best things about being a teenager, some of these relationships are unhealthy, and even violent. In a nationwide survey, one out of ten high school students reported being physically, sexually, or psychologically abused by a girlfriend or boyfriend.

- **Sexually exploiting younger children.** Teens make up almost forty percent of sexual offenders against younger children. Early adolescence (between 12 and 14) is the peak age for sexually harming younger children.

- **Sexting**—sending sexually explicit photos or videos by cell phone or online—is fairly common among young people. One out of five young people have sent nude images of themselves or their friends, sometimes with dire consequences. Teens have faced charges for sending explicit images, which are classified as child pornography by law. There have also been tragic cases of teens committing suicide after their "sexts," originally sent to close friends, got circulated around their schools and beyond.

- *"Hooking up" with online predators.* The Internet is an ideal way for sexual abusers to hook up with young teens. Their victims are usually teenage girls between the ages of 13 and 15. A recent national survey found that one out of eight teenagers received unwanted sexual solicitations over the Internet. Fortunately, few teens report actually meeting these "cyber predators" in person, as such meetings can be very dangerous.

What Can Parents Do?

The teenage years can be a difficult time for both kids and parents. What can you do to help protect your teenager from being sexually exploited and from exploiting others?

- *Learn about the dangers* facing this new generation of teenagers.
- *Recognize the warning signs* of sexual abuse and sexual offending behaviors.
- *Talk openly with your child* about healthy relationships and dating rights and responsibilities.
- *Assist your teen to make safe decisions* about connecting romantically.
- *Help your teen become a critical consumer* of today's sexually charged media environment.
- *Do your best to stay connected to your teen.*

Tweens and teens need your guidance and protection; *Safe Connections* will help you provide both. First, let's look at why teenagers are particularly vulnerable to sexual exploitation.

@

ONE

What Makes Teens Vulnerable to Sexual Exploitation?

Adolescence is a time of many changes. Teens look, think, and act differently as they transform from children to adults. This chapter will briefly describe the physical changes happening in their bodies and brains during puberty so that you can understand why some teens find themselves in harmful situations.

Puberty 101

During puberty, kids' bodies don't simply grow; they morph. Within a few years, the physical changes turn boys into men and girls into women. Girls begin changing first, usually starting around age 10, with boys following one to two years later.

Under the influence of the sex hormones, girls' breasts develop and hips widen and they begin to menstruate around age 12. In boys, the testes and penis enlarge, chests expand, shoulders broaden, voices deepen (with the occasional squeak!), and the body takes on a muscular frame. Boys have their first ejaculation around age 13.

For both boys and girls, the biological and physical changes of puberty lead to a flood of emotions, most noticeably a new interest in romantic relationships and sex. Around age 10, both sexes begin to have sexual thoughts and feelings and attractions to others. Sex now seems exciting, fun, and very interesting.

Everyone Notices!

These changes signal to the youths and others that they are becoming sexually mature. No longer perceived as children, we treat teens differently when they begin to look like adults. An adolescent girl's emerging sexuality may become a source of concern for parents who sometimes respond by placing restrictions on her freedom. In contrast, parents often react to these changes in their sons by giving them more independence and freedom. Alarmingly, adults who are attracted to young developing bodies notice these changes too.

No Brakes!

Like their bodies, teenagers' brains are in the midst of huge growth spurts, especially in the prefrontal cortex, the area of the brain responsible for resisting impulses, planning ahead, problem solving, and understanding consequences of one's actions. These cognitive changes unfold slowly, and continue to mature long after puberty is over. In fact, this part of the brain isn't fully developed until the early twenties. This means that teenagers' impulses and emotions develop several years before their abilities to control them.

During adolescence, the prefrontal cortex is in constant battle with the limbic system, the part of the brain that controls the raw emotions, including sex drive and sensation seeking. Those sex hormones running rampant in your adolescent's bloodstream fuel the limbic system and send it into overdrive, at the same time that their "brakes" (prefrontal cortex) aren't working. Your young teen's body is like an Indy 500 race car—turbo-charged engine, fueled by pedal-to-the-metal hormones, but racing without a skilled driver or a working set of brakes.

An overactive limbic system explains why teens seek out (usually with their friends) exciting and intense experiences, like the Dangerous Ds—Drinking, Driving, and Drugs. But why do they take sexual risks? Because they're on a quest—searching for self-identity; in particular, their own sexual identity.

Search for Sexual Identity

Adolescence is a time when identity issues—achieving a sense of self—are most crucial to development. During the teen years young people explore choices in love, work, and religious and political ideology. They strive to discover their identities and roles in life, and to answer the very important developmental question, "Who am I, apart from my parents?" They also struggle with the narrower question, "Who am I as a sexual person?" A sexual identity is an intrinsic part of a young person's self-definition. Sexual identity includes recognizing one's sexual preference—heterosexual, homosexual, bisexual—and a sense of one's attractiveness to others.

Romantic relationships provide many benefits for teens. First and foremost, teens date for fun and recreation. Dating also makes teens more popular with their peers. Romantic partners provide acceptance, companionship, and emotional comfort to weather the storm of adolescence. Dating helps teens explore their sexual identity and prepares them for adult romantic relationships. Through sexual relationships, teens learn how to manage physical and emotional intimacy.

Parenting Tips

1. *Prepare yourself and your child for the changes.* As they approach adolescence, tweens need to know about all the ways their bodies will change—physically, emotionally, spiritually, and cognitively. With teens maturing earlier compared to decades ago, it's important to begin these discussions early—at least by age 10. Some children need to be prepared even earlier, depending on their rate of development. There are plenty of great books and Web sites that can inform you and your teen.

2. *Communicate your values.* When you talk about their developing sexuality, share your values—those life principles that are important to you. Your values function as voices in their heads that help your teens make sexual decisions when you're not there. You might emphasize values such as staying safe, respecting yourself and others, appreciating personal boundaries (your own and others'), and avoiding sexual behaviors that endanger oneself or exploit others.

3. *Be an "ask-able" parent.* Encourage your children to come to you with questions or concerns. Model how to problem solve.

e

TWO

A Parent's Nightmare:
When Your Teen Is Sexually Abused

'Cause when you're fifteen and somebody tells you they love you
You're gonna believe them
And when you're fifteen, don't forget to look before you fall
Taylor Swift, "Fifteen"

As we discussed in chapter 1, the tween and early teen years bring a new interest in romantic relationships and sex. Unfortunately, some adults exploit teens' sexual curiosity and normal needs for affection, intimacy, and companionship. So that parents are informed about this type of exploitation, chapter 2 covers this topic in some detail.

How Often Does It Happen?

There is very limited research on how often adults sexually abuse teens. One national survey of students in grades 7 to 12 found that ten percent of girls and two percent of boys reported that adults had had sex with them.

Who Are the Abusers?

The biggest myth about childhood sexual abuse is that molesters are strangers. Instead, in almost all cases—ninety percent—the offender is someone the teen knows, including relatives, friends of the family, neighbors, and other adults who are in positions of authority. Authority figures can include members of the clergy, medical or mental health professionals, coaches, teachers, and employers. Sex offenders typically offend alone, and are mostly men, but also women, like the cases of female teachers sexually abusing their teenage male students.

Along with teachers, there have also been cases of male coaches sexually abusing teenage boys. In 1999, *Sports Illustrated* described several male coaches who were arrested for sexually abusing athletes involved in sports from baseball to wrestling. Coaches have also sexually abused teenage girls. In 2010, ABC News reported that thirty-six swimming coaches had been banned for life by the USA Swimming organization for molesting and secretly taping dozens of teenage girl swimmers while they were undressing and showering.

There are several commonalities to these and other cases of teens being sexually abused by adults. In the vast majority of cases, abusers are people teens know and trust and who have power and authority over them. In cases of parent–child incest, abusers are already in a position of authority. *Abusers misuse their power, authority, and trust to sexually exploit teens.*

How to Spot a Potential Abuser

Abusers typically lead double lives, one of public respectability and another of private exploitation. There is no typical sex offender profile—offenders come from all racial, religious, economic, age, and ethnic groups. The saying, "You cannot judge a book by its cover" is especially true when it comes to molesters. Abusers can be anyone. It's impossible to identify sexual abusers based on their outward appearance, public behavior, or relationship to your child. They do, however, give clues through their behaviors—actions that reflect a sexual interest in youth. Most abusers carefully select their victims and then go through a process of emotionally and physically "grooming" them.

Grooming

Grooming refers to the techniques or strategies deliberately undertaken to manipulate a child into engaging in sexual behaviors. Through the grooming process, an offender forms a "special" relationship with the child and gains the victim's trust, then slowly and insidiously breaks down personal and physical boundaries to desensitize the child to sexual behaviors, all the while making sure that the victim keeps the sexual activity a secret.

Grooming teens, parents, and organizations. Sex offenders not only groom children but also their families and sometimes the whole community. They are skilled at ingratiating themselves with teens and infiltrating into unsuspecting families and organizations. Grooming of the family or community has a dual purpose: first, to secure the trust and thus cooperation of the parents in gaining access to the child; and second, to reduce the likelihood of discovery by appearing to be "above reproach." Their reputation often enables them to avoid detection. "I was a very successful tutor," one offender said, "and I used that to my advantage. If they didn't come to me they wouldn't pass their exams, so it was a sort of blackmail. I got quite close to the parents, and the [victims] would see that their parents and I were on good terms and I used that as a lever as well."

A prominent coach who ran an elite girls' basketball program told parents that with his help, their daughters would win college scholarships. He used their dreams of college scholarships to bribe the girls into having sex. He also groomed the parents as effectively as he groomed the teens. One girl remembered sneaking out to a party only to have the coach inform her parents about it. She got punished while he earned their trust. Many parents were proud that their daughters were chosen by this influential coach.

Gaining the teen's sexual compliance. Abusers employ a variety of strategies to get teens to comply with their sexual requests. First, they cultivate a "special" friendship, charming kids with compliments, gifts, and attention to gain the teen's trust and confidence. One 29-year-old female math teacher and coach sexually abused Donna, a 12-year-old straight-A student. The coach spent months gaining Donna's trust, talking to her about her sense of "not belonging" in her family, her feeling unloved by her parents and misunderstood by friends. According to Donna, "She made me feel special, as though I was worth spending time with. She was very interested in what I had to say and really seemed to listen. She'd buy me things: shoes, stuffed animals, and meals. She set up a bank account for my university education and paid for a creative writing course my parents couldn't afford. She said all of these were just her way of helping out, and showing how much she loved me and how much I meant to her."

Sometimes grooming involves flattery. One young athlete said this about his abusing coach, "I was totally flattered that this smart worldly man was taking an interest in me. He spent a lot of time flattering me about my looks and my hockey skills. He was always there by my side, watching me, criticizing me, flattering me, trying to make me love him."

Engaging a child in sexual activities requires privacy, so the offender arranges to be alone with a teen. An offender might ask the teen to go to the movies, offer after-school help, take the teen shopping or out to eat, or offer rides to or from activities. A football coach offered to baby-sit one couple's 13-year-old football-player son so the parents could go out to celebrate their wedding anniversary. While the parents were out, he molested their son.

The time, attention, flattery, and gifts are all ways to emotionally seduce the teen. By bestowing lots of "love" on the child, the child comes to the point where he or she will do anything for the abuser. By spending time alone and developing an exclusive relationship, the teen is effectively cut off from peers and family members—people who could be a source of safety and who could potentially stop the exploitation before the abuser takes it to the next step, that of violating personal boundaries.

Violating boundaries. Through a process of gradual desensitization, the relationship becomes sexualized. The offender begins to blur the boundaries between appropriate and inappropriate touches and talk.

Children are rarely aware they are being groomed. One victim reported, "I didn't know there was anything wrong with [his touching] because I didn't know it was abuse until later. I thought he was showing me affection." Another teen recalled, "It took me forever to figure out what was going on. He called it 'roughhousing' and wanted to do it every time he was alone with me. In summer camp, that happened to be a lot of times. When I got older, I realized he was having erections when he rolled all over me."

Like touches, conversations can cross over into personal and inappropriate territory. The abuser might begin sharing personal matters and introducing sexual topics into conversations. Months before 11-year-old Heather was molested by her 35-year-old computer science teacher, she told her parents that he had started asking her personal questions, like "Are you ever alone at home?" and "Would you like to come camping with me sometime?" Other abusers describe their own sexual experiences or "teach" the teen about sex.

Sometimes offenders show their victims pornographic pictures or Web sites, or take sexual photos or videos of themselves or the child as a way to reduce the teen's resistance. Alcohol, drugs, or marijuana are often used to lower the teen's inhibitions. Others send racy e-mails and text messages. In 2010 an assistant high school principal was arrested for sending a topless photo of herself to a 14-year-old boy. It's not that hard to gain young adolescents' sexual compliance, given their natural curiosity about sex, struggles about sexual identity, insecurity about attractiveness, quest for independence, and desire for romantic connections.

Keeping the Secret: Why Don't Teens Tell?

The grooming process is extremely effective in keeping teens silent. A complex range of emotions—feelings of complicity, embarrassment, betrayal, guilt, shame—all conspire to silence teens and keep them from disclosing the abuse.

Fear. Because of the power abusers hold over teens, it's very difficult to refuse their sexual advances. "He was the coach; I was afraid to say no," one victim of a basketball coach reported. When the girl tried to refuse the coach's advances, he replied, "OK, I don't want to play basketball with you anymore. You won't get into college—I'll make sure of it." Teen victims of coaches are also aware that if they break rank, they could threaten the whole team's success. With their cognitive capacity to imagine the effects of disclosing on their family, team, or community, young teens are vulnerable to being trapped in the offender's web of secrecy. One teen girl believed that if she told about her step-father molesting her, she would be responsible for breaking up her family and that her younger sister would then have to grow up without a father. An adolescent male victim of clergy sexual abuse reported, "I knew it was wrong, but Father Joe said that the whole church could fall apart if people knew."

Concern for the abuser. Sometimes teens don't tell because they like (or "love") the person and don't want the relationship to end or to get the abuser (or themselves) in trouble. An incest survivor explained why she never told about her father abusing her: "My father was all I had. As destructive and as soul murdering as his attention was at night, it was the only attention I received. To believe that my father never loved me during the day, that he only used me for his own pleasures at night, would be to feel a sense of abandonment so deep, so agonizing, it would have destroyed me completely."

Guilt. Teens also keep the secret because they may have disobeyed their parents by being with the offender. And some victims blame themselves, especially if they enjoyed the sexual experience, thinking their natural sexual arousal means they are guilty too.

Shame. Boys seem to have an especially difficult time disclosing. When their abusers are men, boys are reluctant to tell out of embarrassment or fears of being labeled as homosexual. One boy reported that his abusing coach constantly used the threat of revealing him as homosexual to ensure his silence. "I was afraid that if I told, I would have been shut up and sent home, the other players would call me gay and shun me, my hockey career finished." Experts on clergy-perpetrated sexual abuse note that it's particularly difficult for altar boys to tell, when their religion views homosexuality as a sin. Boys sexually exploited by women may not view their experiences as abuse.

How can you use this information to protect your teen from being sexually exploited? Here are some behavioral warning signs that an adult may be grooming your teen.

Warning Signs of Potential Abusers of Teens
Be on the lookout for an adult who:
- gives your teen gifts,
- seems inappropriately physical with children and teens (caressing, wrestling, tickling),

- talks about personal matters with your teen via mobile phone or text messaging,
- offers to spend time alone with your teen outside of work-related responsibilities,
- sends sexually explicit text messages or photos to your teen, or is requesting that your teen do the same,
- singles out your child for a relationship or special attention,
- socializes with kids/teens outside of sanctioned activities,
- purchases drugs, alcohol, or marijuana for youth,
- allows teens to do questionable or inappropriate activities,
- asks teens to keep secrets from parents,
- shares or asks your teen about inappropriate private information,
- your teen talks a lot about his or her "special friend," but when you ask for details about their relationship, he or she gets defensive.

Parenting Tips

1. ***Talk about who sexually exploits teens.*** Accurately describe offenders and how they sexually exploit teens. You might start by defining sexual exploitation. ("It's when one person uses another person to get something sexual, without regard for that person's feelings or safety.") Stress that sexual contact between an adult and a minor is a crime, even if the child is willing, since minors are legally incapable of consenting to sexual activities with adults. Explain that offenders are most likely to be family members, acquaintances, and authority figures.

2. ***Describe grooming.*** Use some of the cases of adult perpetrators presented in this chapter or in media reports to help your teen understand how adults can exploit teenagers' sexual curiosity and take advantage of their normal needs for affection, intimacy, and companionship. Help your teen understand how it can feel flattering or exciting when an adult takes an interest in them. Describe what you consider inappropriate behavior or violations of boundaries by an authority figure (for example, improper touching, showing them pornographic material, talking to them about sexuality, constantly texting or calling).

3. *Point out warning signs.* Describe how offenders violate boundaries, both in conversations and touches. Point out red flags, like "sexting," being asked personal questions, or talking about sex. Alert your teen that if an authority figure says, "Do not tell your parents or anyone" about the relationship, the first thing the teen should do is to tell you or another safe adult.

4. *Create a safety plan.* Make sure your child knows how to resist an offender's sexual advances. You might say, "You are a special person who deserves to be treated with respect and not to be abused—physically, emotionally, or sexually. No one has the right to force, threaten, or trick you into having sex of any kind. If someone tries to push you into doing something sexual, try to get away from the person and then tell me or another trusted adult." Generate a list of safe adults to whom your child could turn for support. Emphasize that, "Even if you cannot stop the person, it is never your fault. Sexual abuse is always the responsibility of the abuser."

5. *Don't fall for flattery yourself.* You may feel flattered when an authority figure shows interest in your child, especially someone who is held in high regard or who promises to make your child a star. Try to see beyond this "interest" and trust your intuition. If this person seems too good to be true, he or she probably is. Also, encourage teens to trust their instincts if they are uncomfortable with or have suspicions about a person.

6. *Monitor and screen your teen's activities and companions.* As much as possible, monitor the whereabouts of your teens—know where they are, what they are doing, and with whom. Before allowing your child to participate in extracurricular activities (sporting leagues, youth clubs, faith-based groups, scouting) ask the directors of the youth-serving organization what they are doing to protect children from sexual victimization. For example, are screening and background checks conducted on all volunteers and employees? Does the organization require all staff and volunteers to sign a Code of Conduct specifying acceptable and unacceptable behaviors with children? Ask if there are poli-

cies prohibiting adult–teen interactions outside of organization-sanctioned activities and programs. Never allow your teen to socialize or spend the night alone with any authority figure from a youth-serving organization. Ask sports coaches what the arrangements are for showering after practices and for sleeping on road trips. It may be challenging, inconvenient, or embarrassing to question authority figures about your child's safety, but your extra effort will go far in protecting your child.

7. *Screen your own companions.* Some molesters develop romantic relationships with single mothers to gain unlimited access to their children. As a single parent, how can you make careful decisions about whom to invite into your home and to possibly share parenting duties? First, take the time to get to know your new friend well before introducing him or her to your children. Second, be alert to any of the warning signs you learned in this chapter that the person might have a sexual interest in your children. If you need help breaking off the relationship, seek assistance from a counselor or law enforcement officer.

8. *Help your teen help a friend.* Your child may need to help a friend (or family member) who has been sexually exploited. Teens are more likely to confide in their friends than adults if they are being sexually abused. Brainstorm ways your teen could help, such as:

- Believe them. People rarely lie about sexual abuse.

- Reassure your friend that the abuse was NOT their fault. Even if they took "stupid" risks like being alone with the person after their parents forbade them to do so.

- Encourage your friend to tell an adult, so that your friend can get help and the offender does not abuse anyone else. Offer to go with your friend to talk to a counselor, doctor, faith leader, or police officer. (Be sure your teen knows that even if their friend refuses to report, your child must tell an adult, even if it means losing a friendship. The friend's safety is more important.)

- Do not offer to confront or beat up the offender. It may get you hurt or in trouble with the law, and will only make matters worse.

• Keep the information confidential. Do help your friend tell an adult who can help. But don't tell other friends or classmates—don't betray your friend's trust.

Tweens and teens can be sexually exploited anytime they are alone with a sexual abuser who has power and authority over them. The next chapter describes sexual abuse occurring in cyberspace. The Internet is an ideal way for abusers to initiate sexual relationships with youths. It provides access to countless teens in a relatively anonymous environment (the perfect opportunity for privacy).

@

THREE

Help Your Teen Make Safe Online Connections

"She was great. I felt I could talk with her about anything. Like she was my best friend. When I met her, 'she' turned out to be 'he' and was much older than me. He frightened and hurt me."
Thirteen-year-old boy who met his chat room friend offline

"I met him through a chat room. He said he ran a model agency and needed more models. He got me to send pictures of myself and told me I was beautiful. . . . I was really excited. It felt like I'd known him for ages and we fixed to meet up. I'm just so glad I took my friend with me because it turned out that he wasn't who he said he was—he yelled at me for bringing my friend and then just left us."
Fourteen-year-old girl groomed through a chat room

The Internet is a wonderful resource and teaching tool for everyone—children, teens, and adults. Teens use it to research topics for school, play games, watch videos, listen to music, get health and medical information, shop, and connect socially with family members, school friends, and people around the world.

However, the Internet also poses a variety of risks for teen users. There are risks related to your family's safety and security, unwanted exposure to sexual material, the risks of criminal charges for sending sexually explicit pictures, and the potential for contact with cyber sexual predators.

Characteristics of Online Offenders

Similar to in-person offending, most cyber sexual abusers are males. Online offenders are most likely peers, friends of the family, acquaintances, relatives, or neighbors. What kinds of teens do they target?

Almost all victims are between 13 and 17 years old. Most are either 13 or 14. Girls are at higher risk, but one-fourth of victims are boys. Boys who are gay or questioning their sexual orientation are especially vulnerable to online victimization. Cyber predators also target certain at-risk teens—those who appear especially needy, lonely, worried about their appearance or popularity, or alienated from parents and friends.

There are some risky online behaviors that make certain teens more likely to be targeted. These include making rude or nasty comments (called "flaming"), using profanity or obscene language, embarrassing or bullying others, and discussing sex, especially in chat rooms. Youths who visit chat rooms are more at risk for receiving sexual solicitations. Offenders also look for certain kinds of personal profiles on social-networking sites like MySpace, Facebook, and Twitter. Online predators target teens who use sexually suggestive screen names (HOTTIE4U) or when names include ages (FLIRTYGRL14). Predators also approach teens who post sexually provocative pictures (like posing in swimsuits or underwear) or blog about sexual activity.

Online Grooming

Online grooming occurs when an offender contacts a youth and establishes a relationship by claiming to have similar interests and activities. He might offer a sympathetic "ear" to the teen's concerns (perhaps about school problems, boyfriend or girlfriend issues, or parent conflict). Over time, the predator gains the affection, interest, and trust of the teen.

As part of this grooming process, the online predator might send naked pictures of himself. He does this to desensitize the teen to sexual material. Or the teen is asked to send sexual pictures or sexually explicit videos of him- or herself. Sexual solicitation can also involve sexual talk or invitations to engage in sexual activity. When the perpetrator has gained the teen's trust, then the predator arranges to get together in person, with the intent to have sex. In one recent case, a 15-year-old girl from California met a 32-year-old man online who claimed to be in the entertainment industry and could help her "get a break." After talking online for months through MySpace, he flew her from California to Florida, picked her up at the airport, drove her to a nearby apartment, and raped her.

Warning Signs of Possible Cyber Sexual Exploitation

- Your teen spends large amounts of time online, especially at night.
- Your teen becomes secretive about online activity, for example, turning the computer monitor off or quickly changing the screen when you come into the room.
- You find evidence of your teen sending and receiving sexually explicit images or messages on cell phones or computers.
- Your teen receives mail, gifts, or packages from strangers.
- Your teen receives phone calls from adults you don't know or is making calls, sometimes long distance, to numbers you don't recognize. Check your phone bills (home phones and your teen's cell phone) for excessive calls, text messages, and long-distance calls.

Parenting Tips

1. ***Good parent–child communication*** is the number one safety tip for cyberspace, as for anywhere else. Talk to your teen often about her online experiences, just like you do with her offline ones. Spend time online with your teen so that you can learn about his interests and activities. Know the Web sites and chat rooms your teen visits. Check your computer's browser history to learn which sites your teen is visiting. What do their social profiles reveal about them—too much? Become acquainted with your teen's online friends the same way you get to know her school friends. As often as you can, accompany teens while they surf the Internet.

2. ***Teach kids to be good citizens*** and respectful of others online as much as offline. Do not rely exclusively on safety software to protect your children from cyber predators. Installing security software, filters, and monitors can certainly help; however, it is more important that you describe how cyber predators operate and encourage your teen to avoid risky online behaviors. Kids who are aggressive and mean online are at greater risk of becoming victims themselves.

3. ***Be sure your teen uses a safe screen name,*** one that doesn't reveal their age or gender and isn't sexually suggestive.

4. ***Talk to your teen about the risks of making sexual statements*** or engaging in "sex talk" online, especially in chat rooms. Certain chat rooms are designed just for kids, and are usually monitored to make sure content is "kid-safe." Warn your teen that unmonitored and public chat rooms are usually filled with strangers who might be "eavesdropping" on their conversations. Require that your teen check with you first before joining public chat rooms.

5. ***Discuss with your teen the online grooming tactics*** used by cyber predators. Encourage teens to be as alert online as offline for possible manipulation or exploitation. Help them understand how some adults will exploit a teen's sexual curiosity and needs for comfort and intimacy. Make it clear that just as in the

real world, there are people in cyberspace who try to make sexual connections with teens. Make sure they know that along with strangers, family members and acquaintances also use the Internet to sexually offend.

6. **Help your teen develop critical thinking skills** so he can make safe decisions in cyberspace. Propose "what if?" questions specific to Internet safety. You might ask, "What if your online 'friend' asks you to use your webcam to tape you doing something sexual?" or "What if a new online 'friend' wanted to meet you in person?" Only allow face-to-face meetings if you (or another trusted adult) can accompany your teen and if the meeting is in a safe public location. Share this chapter's examples of teens who have been victims of Internet predators.

7. **Explain to your teen that it's a crime for adults to use the Internet** to make sexual advances or send sexual material to minors. Brainstorm with your teens what to do if they ever receive sexual material or messages from someone online. ("Log off if someone makes you uncomfortable or asks you to do something that is wrong. Write down the username of that person so we can contact operators of the chat room, our Internet service provider, or report it to the Cyber Tipline at (800) 843-5678 or at www.cybertipline.com.")

8. **Encourage your child to think before sending or posting a personal picture or video.** Tell him or her to ask, "Would I mind if my parent, grandparent, or a future employer saw it?" before hitting send. Make sure your teen knows it's illegal to send or post nude or sexually suggestive photos or videos of themselves or their friends via mobile phones or the Web. Explain that "if you send or forward the picture, you can be charged with a felony—production or distribution of child pornography. If you keep it on your phone or computer, you can be charged with possession of child pornography. In some cases you could even end up on a sex offender registry." Along with legal consequences, sexting has moral consequences—being disrespectful of another and violating a friend's trust. What should they do if a friend sends them

a nude or semi-nude image of a classmate? Experts recommend immediately deleting the image, then telling the friend to stop sending those kinds of images. Make sure the friend knows that sexting is against the law. If the photos keep coming, ask your teen to tell you and you may need to talk with the friend's parents, school authorities, or the police.

9. *Make sure you've been granted access to teens' social networking sites* so you can monitor their online activity—the images they're posting, who they are talking to, and what information they're revealing about themselves. You're not invading their privacy if they're putting personal information and images in public online places. Remind your child that the images they post online can have consequences offline. Employers, college admissions officers, coaches, teachers, and the police may view your child's posts.

10. *Help your teen reveal a friend's sexual involvement* with an adult online to a parent or trusted adult to prevent the friend's victimization.

11. *Discuss appropriate and inappropriate uses of these devices* before purchasing new technologies (computers, webcams, digital cameras, mobile phones) for your teen. Together with your teen, decide on the terms and conditions for their use.

12. *Be alert to behavior* that may mean your teen is being groomed by an online predator.

By taking an active role in your teen's Internet activities, you'll be ensuring that your child can benefit from the wealth of valuable information the Internet has to offer, without being exposed to its potential dangers.

e

FOUR

When Teens Offend

The idea that your teen might cause harm to another child or teenager is so shameful, it's easier for most parents to deny that possibility and skip this chapter. Please don't. The only way childhood sexual abuse is ever going to be eliminated is if we give young people guidelines for sexually respectful boundaries with others, including younger children and their dating partners. No easy task given our sexually disrespectful society!

Youth Who Sexually Harm Younger Children

It may surprise you to learn that teenagers (mostly boys, but also girls) sexually abuse younger children. In fact, almost half (forty percent) of all child sexual offenders are teenagers. Victims can include their siblings and cousins (called incest) along with children in their care (for example, while baby-sitting).

Most adult child sexual offenders report that they first started sexually abusing children while they were teenagers between 12 and 14 years of age. As you learned in chapter 1, this is the time when teens' interest in sexuality is very high, yet they often lack the "brakes" to keep their impulses in check.

Common Traits of Adolescent
Sexual Offenders
Risks of sexually abusing young children
increase for teens who:
- have a strong sense of entitlement (believe that rules don't apply to them and that they can do whatever they want without regard for others' feelings),
- are impulsive or have problems delaying gratification,

• lack good judgment, planning, and problem-solving skills,
• are socially awkward or anxious, or lack good social skills,
• have learning difficulties or other problems at school (e.g., disruptive behavior, truancy),
• have a history of rule breaking (e.g., delinquency, stealing, fighting, property damage),
• have a history of harming others (e.g., bullying younger children or hurting animals),
• have a history of problematic sexual behaviors (e.g., masturbating in public, voyeurism, obscene phone calls, exhibitionism),
• use alcohol or drugs,
• have low self-esteem or are depressed,
• lack empathy for others (focus on their needs, not on others').

Why Do Adolescents Sexually Exploit Younger Children?

As explained in chapter 1, both boys and girls begin to have sexual thoughts, feelings, and arousal during the early teen years. They are naturally curious about sex. To satisfy their sexual curiosity, some teenage baby-sitters use the child care opportunity to experiment with sex. Other teenagers use children to meet their intimacy needs. Some teens want to be close to others, but may lack social skills or opportunities for interacting with boys or girls their age or they fear being rejected by them. Should they also experience high levels of sexual thoughts, fantasies, and arousal, they might take advantage of younger children to meet their sexual and emotional needs. Others misuse their superior size and power to force younger children to comply. Another factor that can contribute to sexually offending behavior is when a child has experienced sexual abuse. Children who have been sexually abused sometimes react by forcing younger children into the same kind of sexual behavior. Teens who view degrading or violent sexually explicit materials (in magazines, Web sites, or video games) also learn how to sexually exploit others.

Some teens do not know that being sexual with a child is immoral, illegal, or harmful. In her book, *Protecting Your Children from Sexual Predators,* Leigh Baker quotes this adolescent offender, "I knew what I was doing to my sister was wrong, and that my mother would be very angry at me if she found out. But I thought that getting in deep trouble with my mom would be the most that would happen. I never knew that I could get in trouble with the law for what I did." Another 15-year-old boy didn't know that sexually offending his 7-year-old female cousin was wrong. His parents had taught him not to get sexually involved with teenage girls, and since she was not a teenager, he didn't think it was wrong.

Parenting Tips

1. *Rights to privacy.* In your home, emphasize that each family member has the right to privacy or times and places where they can be alone. All family members should be entitled to privacy when they are bathing, dressing, sleeping, using the toilet, and doing other personal activities. When family members do not respect each other's privacy, physical boundaries can be crossed, and the risk for sexual abuse increases.

2. *Teach body ownership.* You can teach your children from a young age the concept that "I'm the boss of my body!" and that they are in charge of keeping their bodies safe. Teenagers with a healthy concept of body ownership appreciate their own bodies and know they have the right to refuse unsafe and, especially, secret touches of their bodies. They also take responsibility for keeping themselves safe in many situations, for protecting their sexual and reproductive health, and for avoiding sexual behaviors that are harmful to themselves or others.

3. *Establish baby-sitting ground rules.* Before allowing teens to supervise younger children (whether a family member or someone else's child), review body-safety rules they must follow to keep themselves, as well as the children they supervise, safe. If appropriate, cover sexually safe, respectful diapering and bathing of younger children. Make sure your teen knows that sexual contact with children is abuse, not play, and that it is a crime and harms children.

4. Help your teen develop empathy. Taking care of younger children, animals, or the elderly (under supervision) can offer opportunities for adolescents to learn how to be respectful and protective of others who have less power or are more vulnerable. Child sex offenders usually lack such traits as respect, honesty, self-control, and empathy. Help your children develop these important pro-social traits by teaching them from an early age how to treat others.

Adolescents Who Abuse Their Dating Partners

Dating violence is a serious problem in the United States. Studies have shown that alarming numbers of teens report being verbally, physically, emotionally, or sexually abused by a dating partner. Nationally, about ten percent of students say they have been physically hurt by a boyfriend or girlfriend in the past year. A large number of teens report being pressured, threatened, or forced to do something sexual with a current or former dating partner.

After hearing heart-breaking testimony from parents whose daughters were killed by their boyfriends, Congress declared February to be "National Teen Dating Violence Awareness and Prevention Month." Parents need to be aware of how often teens are harmed by their romantic partners, understand that girls are as likely as boys to perpetrate partner violence, know the warning signs of teen dating violence, and how to talk to their sons and daughters to prevent them from becoming victims or perpetrators of dating abuse.

Parenting Tips

1. Talk openly about dating rights and responsibilities. Just like driving a car, dating is a privilege that comes with both rights and responsibilities. Your teen's asking for permission to date presents a perfect opportunity for you to talk about expectations for dating relationships. This is an ideal time to promote healthy relationships and prevent patterns of dating violence that can last a lifetime. Together with your teen, decide on the terms and conditions under which your teen is allowed to date.

2. *Model how to have a healthy, respectful relationship* with your own partner. Through the way you and your partner treat each other, your teen will learn what it means to have a healthy romantic relationship, free from harm and full of respect.

3. *Demonstrate respectful touching with your teen.* Touching and being affectionate to loved ones is a good way to show love. It's important that daughters and sons have parents who can be affectionate but who also honor their requests to stop. Teens may start refusing your affectionate hugs and kisses in their effort to pull away from you and be "grown up." If your teen's refusal seems more than the typical teen embarrassment, it could indicate that your teen is experiencing dating violence or sexual exploitation. Share your concerns with your teen and ask if he or she would like to talk to you or another trusted adult about their experiences. Most importantly, your teen must know that no matter what the circumstances, abuse is never the teen's fault.

4. *Know the warning signs of dating abuse.* An abusive partner is one who does any or all of the following:

   • Calls his or her partner names or insults them in front of others.

   • Texts or calls the partner excessively.

   • Gets jealous or angry when the partner spends time with others.

   • Is possessive, and tries to control where the partner goes, how they dress, who they hang with or talk to. "My boyfriend has complete control of the relationship," one young teen disclosed. "I have at least thirty rules that I have to follow. I have body jewelry and I can't wear any of that and I can't wear skirts. He won't let me go out with my friends. He said it was because he loved me and he didn't want anyone else to have me."

   • Threatens to kill or hurt their partner or themselves if the partner tries to end the relationship.

   • Hits, slaps, pushes, kicks, or forces the partner to have sex.

e

FIVE

Raising Sexually Respectful Teens in a Sexually Disrespectful World

Parents play key roles in helping their children become sexually respectful and responsible adults. Teens who do not get information from their parents will learn about sexuality from friends and mass media, television, video games, music, magazines, movies, and the Internet. Much of this information is inaccurate, even harmful.

The World Wide Web is an especially dangerous sex educator for youth. In a survey of American teens, forty-two percent (mostly boys) said they had viewed sexually explicit Web sites while surfing the Internet. On these X-rated or pornographic sites, teens are exposed to models of sexuality that are often disrespectful, brutal, and violent. Pornography gives teenagers the idea that women and girls are sexual objects, to be used at their will.

Teens are caught in a cross fire of mixed messages about sexuality. Parents often express disapproval of sex at young ages and outside of marriage, yet the media portrays casual sex as fun and exciting, without any negative consequences. And the messages are different for boys and girls. Boys are expected to be sexual aggressors, unable to control themselves. For girls especially, sex is seen as a way to become popular. Girls are being told from young ages to look and act "sexy" and to use the power of sex to attract boys.

What Can Parents Do to Fight Back?

- Be aware of how many sexual messages are bombarding your children. They're everywhere—on the radio, TV, DVDs, video games,

Internet, magazines, billboards, and clothing. Fight against the toy and clothing producers who sexualize small children. "You should be ashamed!" one critic posted on the Abercrombie & Fitch Web site, after it offered padded bikini tops for tween girls.

• Help your teens recognize the cultural forces shaping their views on sexuality. Join your teen in watching movies and television. Afterwards, count how many times you see people using sex to manipulate others. Ask your teen, "What is healthy/unhealthy about this relationship?"

Listen to their favorite songs or watch music videos together. Decode the messages being sent through clothing, dance, and gestures about gender, relationships, and sexuality. What do the lyrics of the song mean?

Look at advertisements together, noticing how advertisers use sex to manipulate people into buying their products. Comment on fashion trends—what messages do they send to others? Use this opportunity to talk about the images they and their friends portray through their clothes, make-up, jewelry, tattoos, hair, etc.

Examine news reports about adults who act in sexually disrespectful ways. Help your teen see how the offender took advantage of a vulnerable person to meet his or her sexual needs. Use these teachable moments to share your view that it is never acceptable for someone to use another person for sex.

Teach Teens How to Make Safe Decisions

Because of their "still cooking" brain, teens lack the neurological tools to make good decisions, particularly in the face of incessant sexual bombardment in shows, music, and advertisements. As a parent of a teen with a still-developing prefrontal cortex, your job will be to assist in the "brain training," and help your son or daughter learn good decision-making skills. Here are some ways to do that:

• *Teach and model through your own behavior* how to make good decisions and solve problems. Share with them how you weigh options, risks and benefits, implications, and consequences of any action you're considering.

- *Try to listen without judging your child* should your teen share a problem or concern with you. Let teens know how proud or glad you are that they came to you to talk about the problem. Ask what they feel or think about the situation, and what options and solutions they've considered. Encourage your child to consider more than one solution to any problem, and then narrow down the choices by looking at the pros and cons of each.

- *Explain how changes in their brains,* combined with peer pressure along with drugs and alcohol, can increase the risk of impulsive actions. Help them understand how hard it is to say "no" to sexual activities when their "brakes" aren't working and their bodies are saying "yes." Help them plan for how they want to respond in sexual situations so they are prepared if and when the time comes.

- *Create opportunities for your teens to talk about their lives* (for example, during dinner, while doing dishes or washing the car; driving alone with your teen or while carpooling their friends). Appeal directly to your teenager's self-centeredness. Asking questions that tap into feelings, thoughts, or opinions makes your teen feel important and strengthens your connection. And always make sure to listen more than you talk.

Reach Out to Other Parents

This is hard work, staying connected to these complicated creatures while they try to distance themselves from you. Many parents benefit from the support of others. Talk to your partner or friends, reach out to extended family, or join parent support groups. Form online parenting groups. Whether online or face-to-face, having a network of support can help you navigate the storm of adolescence.

Although the world has changed, what tweens and teens need from their parents hasn't. New millennium teens still need respect, emotional support, encouragement to grow and make their own decisions, open and honest communication, and connection with caring adults and peers. Teens will survive and thrive when they have parents and other caring adults who provide them with warmth, safety, and most important, love.

℮

Index